Between Storms

Between Storms

Carol V. Davis

Carol V. Davis

For Leonora,

Poetry lover!

Carol V. Davis

9.6.13

New Odyssey Series
Truman State University Press
Kirksville, Missouri

tsup.truman.edu

Cover art: Neil Meitzler, *Untitled*, ca. 1964.
Cover design: Teresa Wheeler

Library of Congress Cataloging-in-Publication Data

Davis, Carol V.
Between storms / Carol V. Davis.
p. cm.
ISBN 978-1-61248-054-1 (pbk. : alk. paper) — ISBN 978-1-61248-055-8 (ebook)
I. Title.
PS3604.A9558B48 2012
811'.6—dc23

2011049719

The paper in this publication meets or exceeds the minimum requirements of the American National Standard for Information Sciences—Permanence of Paper for Printed Library Materials, ANSI Z39.48–1992.

In memory of Louis Elkin Davis and Edith Kaufman Davis
and of Jonathan Franklin Davis

I went out into the night and nothing was ever the same.

—Judith Kitchen

Contents

Acknowledgments

Grateful acknowledgment is made to the editors of the following journals in which poems in this collection first appeared, sometimes in different versions.

Agenda (London): "Merce Cunningham and the Music" and "The Closing"
Ars Interpres (Stockholm): "The Black of Everything" and "Pairing the Animals"
Bridges: "The Statue"
Calyx: "Bruges"
Cider Press Review: "Each Time the Doors Open" and "Plumeria"
Chiron Review: "Fire Ant"
The Dos Passos Review: "Defying Gravity"
Hayden's Ferry Review: "Bleak with Trees"
The Los Angeles Review: "Instruction in Witchcraft"
Natural Bridge: "With No Definite End"
Nimrod: "The Spiral," "Roots," and "The Art of the Stitch"
Pebble Lake: "The Anatomy of a Palm and the Confluence of Lines"
Permafrost: "Mockingbird II"
Poet Lore: "The Way Light Begins to Fold on Itself"
Ploughshares: "Eating Crow" and "Marshland"
Prairie Schooner: "Carnation, Lily, Lily, Rose"
The Prose-Poem Project: "Chocolate and the Afterlife"
Quiddity: "Bindweed" and "Between Storms"
The Reprint: "Carnation, Lily, Lily, Rose"
Revival Poetry Journal (Ireland): "The Icon Painter" and "The Insomniac"
ripple(s): "Gnats"
Slipstream: "Voices"
The South Carolina Review: "Summer of Love"
The Truth About the Facts: "New Math"
Verdad: "Copper and Steel" (published as "Loving a Plumber")

Waterhouse Review (Scotland): "Driving Late at Night in Hollywood with a Foreign Visitor"
Women in Judaism: A Multidisciplinary Journal (Toronto): "Leonard Bernstein Speaks to Me"

"Laundromat" appeared in *Lavandaria: A Mixed Load of Women, Wash, and Word* (2009); "Fear II" in *Illness & Grace, Terror & Transformation* (2007); "New Math" in *Butterfly Away,* Magnapoets Anthology Series 3 (2011). "The Way Light Begins to Fold on Itself" received the 2009 DA Center for the Arts Poetry Prize.

I am grateful to the Jentel Arts Foundation for the generous support that enabled the writing of some of these poems, and to Olivet College for inviting me to be Poet-in-Residence there. Thank you to Ailish Hopper and Andrea Carter Brown for their invaluable help and, as always, to Peggy Aylsworth Levine. I am grateful to Peter and Aimee Frazier for permission to use the Neil Meitzler painting on the cover. And deepest appreciation to Nancy Rediger, director of Truman State University Press, for her support, patience, and unwavering belief in poetry.

I

Marshland

We are all intruders here
        though we fool ourselves this late winter day,
carving a place on the banks
                to anchor our heels.
We stretch over the water, hoping
        to slip onto the wings of a great blue heron
but afraid to get caught in the trap of reeds, twisting
                in the foul water.
The marsh ignites: will-o'-the-wisps,
                sprites, a wisp of flames,
torches held aloft by villagers
        marching on the manor.
We've read too many fairy tales
                but this much is true:
I heard voices.
        Not the call of a willet or clapper rail
but a child caught beneath the ceiling of water
                the thin reed of its voice
rising in the brackish light.

Roots

I keep returning
to the gnarly roots of things:

nuggets of words freed
from their appendages

In Russian
a verb depends on its prefix:

Choose carefully for with one
you can make it home on the

St. Petersburg metro
before it halts at one a.m. to allow

the 500+ bridges to yawn open
so the hulking freighters can

slink into harbor
before the captain finishes the last dregs of vodka

Choose the other prefix and
You'll be gazing out of the rickety tram

that sighs at every turn of track
as it sways out of the city on a late fall afternoon

If you're lucky you'll make it
before sundown—the perfect time to forage

for mushrooms in the very forest where
the partisans hid, bits of song escaping over the treetops

It is cold by California standards
I burrow elbow deep in a cardboard box

grasping for that perfect
knot of bulb that promises a red tulip

come spring and so much more

Voices

At ten she opened the second-story window
of their Tulsa house and in they flew.

Though she did not understand, she gathered them.

Her great aunt too had heard such voices,
but learned early to fold her hands in class.

The war years, one should not appear different.

Now in a city that spills into the ocean,
threatened by fire and earthquake,

my friend lives by a cemetery, walks between graves.

At night she opens her porch door:
a girl with tattered sleeves drifts in. Shadows
condense into a woman
who strikes a fire, which threatens the curtains.

In the cemetery the voices crouch in the gathering fog
whispering to her.
A hot wind sets the teeth on edge

Stone sentries leave their posts, goose-step on either side of her
as she picks her way between the mossy graves.

She searches for a headstone carved with scrolls.
She must read this for names of her enemies.
These are her instructions.
Her one chance to save us, even if we resist.

The Way Light Begins to Fold on Itself

The way light begins to fold on itself,
an accordion of white and gray.

A late morning between storms,
but it could be near dusk.

That was the color of the air.
The hour between one lashing rain and the next.

You could smell the uncertainty,
a bitter nut or bark peeling, saffron or something unnamable.

No one would be surprised if a spouse
walked out the door, clicking it shut and not returning.

Soon a hiss announced the next storm's entrance.
You could imagine the lifted bows of a string section

waiting for the conductor: the first measures tentative
before the curtain opens with the hefty soprano rooted in place.

The taunting mockingbirds on the phone wire
dared any other creature to remain outside.

The lamps shuddered in warning,
enough so you knew to be afraid.

Pairing the Animals

Watching my cats tumble
like the fury of a riptide,
I know the usual pairings
would never work.
The lions would tear
each other to strips of rag,
the mourning doves collapse
in a puddle of grief.
We must start again
with the unlikely:
panther with possum, for
suspicion binds stronger
than love.
Canadian goose with elk.
Both are prepared
for arduous journey.
Who to match
with a woman who aches
with longing?
She stands by the window,
strokes the splintering sill
of the cavernous ark,
staring across the water.

Between Storms

My clunker car inches along
like the tail of a rattler trying
to whip up its fury.
Ahead of me an orange jeep, a copperhead sunning.

A sweep of clouds darkens the sky.
On either side of the traffic
the canyon walls are growing.
The heavens could open now,
lightning bounce from the cheekbones of rocks.
Scrub acorns sprout from the hillsides,
its stubble of beard sways unsteadily.

I did not believe I could bring back the dead,
though now they slide onto the back seat
as I round a sharp corner.
My brother shifts in the bones of his teenage body,
gazes out the window ignoring the conversation.
My mother in matching pumps and purse,
face bright before the illness that took away its color.
My father leans forward, cautions me to slow down.
A red-tailed hawk loops and dips above.
It urges me to follow closely.
The road widens.

Bindweed

A weed is a plant whose virtues have not yet been discovered.
—Ralph Waldo Emerson

Call it morning glory, *Convolvulus arvenis,*
and people smile, thinking of purple suns strung across a field.
Standing on my back stairs this summer morning
I am filled with hate toward this choking vine that can live twenty years.
John Dunmire, expert gardener, cautions that bindweed
can send up one thousand plants in a flower bed,
squatters invading a vegetable garden.
I am in such a fight for life as this noxious vine
strangles rose bushes, Australian myrtle, fuchsias.
It loops across the lawn to bind its phylacteries
around orange tree branches.
For months I wrestle the bindweed, pull its tentacles,
smother its outbursts, starve its roots.
I scream curses enough to scare the gods
(as well as the neighbors), but the plant twists tighter.
And though I fed my children only on the breast,
I dream of herbicides to poison the bindweed's tissue,
brown streaks snaking up its limbs like tetanus.
Its torso shriveling to a gnarled pit.
Let the woody stems be coated, the leafy greens
glimmer with glyphosate. I'll brush on triclopyr,
paint the offshoots with dicamba, leave voodoo dolls at its feet.
Make the bindweed suffer until it pleads with me
to die and be done with it.

Mockingbird II

How perfectly he has mastered
the car alarm, jangling us from sleep.
Later his staccato scatters smaller birds
that landed on the wire beside him.
Perhaps the key to success
is imitation, not originality.
Once when the cat slinked up
the orange tree and snatched a hatchling,
the mockingbird turned on us,
marked us for revenge.
For two whole weeks he dive-bombed
whenever I ventured out the screen door
lured by his call: first tricked into thinking
the soft coo was a mourning dove courting,
next drawn by the war cry of a far larger animal.
He swooped from one splintered eve, his mate from the other,
aiming to peck out my eyes, to wrestle
the baby from my arms, to do God knows what
with that newborn.

With No Definite End

Then it was over, though there was no definite end.
A man walks away in a movie and
does not turn around, even when his fedora
lifts from his head, sailing to the pavement behind him.

*

A man sends her an elaborate box hinged by two brass butterflies
with painted vines winding drunkenly around the sides.
Their primary colors at odds with the winter of its making.
Her roommate insists she send the gift back.

*

The world shrinks to a distillation of sound—
the predawn lament of the mourning dove.
A woman shuts the window,
though the cries continue to reach her.

*

After decades there is much to say, though both parties
are weighted down by too many footnotes.
She has watched many snowfalls from behind glass.
Even on the telephone a father's words can strangle a son.
The sun hisses at its rapid sinking into the sea.

Fear II

My foreign student
calls to say she is afraid

of spiders and what
should she do?

I start to think about fear.
But what I mean to say

is that the face is
on both sides of the window.

And that is why you
must draw the shades.

When I lived
on top of a mountain

the only face
was the white mask

of the unblinking owl
or a smudge on the sill

left as a calling card
by a reclusive cougar.

It is too early to predict
what will happen next.

The dark drops its burden
all night long, deepening

as it empties its buckets
of stars, leaving the expanse

of black on the other side
of the window.

Carnation, Lily, Lily, Rose

after a painting by John Singer Sargent

is not the first painting
I was afraid of.
That distinction belongs
to Hieronymus Bosch,
a melon-round head leering
with a pumpkin's grin.
The body of a lion married
to the feet of a crow.

It is *Carnation, Lily, Lily, Rose*
that frightens me still.
Others take comfort in the innocence
of the mirrored girls in white, ruffled collars.
Those lanterns are not to be trusted;
the orange glow in their bellies
a beacon to the other side.

You can tell me how foolish I am.
It won't be the first time,
but who's to say the white lilies
are not omens of death, the one girl
a ghost of the other?

Darkness

It is not true
                    darkness descends quietly
on a fist of lake

As if a stab of ash
                              the light plunges
                    to extinguish itself
before the water rises
                              to meet it

Later the two remember that night
                    a humming drifted toward shore

Perhaps a quiver of wings
                    or a chorus of children's voices

Beating the water's surface from below

Trapped beneath the lapping shards of waves

And so the dark
                              meets the dark

A kind of hunger
                    in the mixing vat

Let it die down
Let the voices subside
Let the bruised retreat

Gnats

Language tethers us to the world.
—Penelope Lively

This is how it begins.
A darkening, a whining of wings.
With the first cloud of gnats lakeside
I took to slinking home,
key out, ready for the dash to the door.
Soon I am peering through the window slats.
Hadn't I always been an easy target?
Words that belong to me begin to disintegrate.
Verb endings unhook themselves.
I spot them congregating in darkened bars.
Exclamation marks wander the streets as gangs.
I can't catch the whisper of the neighbors,
but their teeth all point in my direction.
When the police car pulls up, I'll be ready.
It's the gnats put them up to it.

Plumeria

for Antoinette

Calm down.
That the moon has always hung
by a thread expecting to be snipped
is a given. Your daughter
will call when she is ready.
There is no need for hysteria.
A beach ball held under water
will always shoot into the crackling air.
No one can stop it.
While you wait, feed the plumeria,
even if its awning is bolted shut for the winter.
You've got to believe in something.
You could do worse than to have faith
in the unfurling of petals.

The Black of Everything

We move between two darknesses.
—E. M. Forester

At first it was the crows
on the checkerboard lawns,
while the block slept.
So still the earth had stopped
its spinning under the grip of talons.
The birds' shrill cries erupted
like a fury of Yemenite tongues
ululating at a funeral.
A lash of wings over the city.
They must be emissaries of the Angel of Death
entombing the sky in their black greatcoats,
then choosing a street to pluck from.
Cancer twice in the odd-numbered houses.
Neighbor children used to be safe here.
Now they cross to the other side
and back again in uncertainty,
as if such a curse were catching,
while today out early to pluck dead petals,
I walk blindly into a smothering of crows.

II

Laundromat

Nothing can brighten this laundromat,
not the fake ivy strung like a clothesline
across its middle, washers on one side,
dryers on the other, nor the framed
jigsaw puzzles under smeared glass.
Germanic villages with steepled churches
and quaint squares tucked sleepily
against the shards of mountains.
Tiles broken and missing, as if the
floor had hosted dance parties after the doors
were locked, the machines' lids lowered.
The twirling stilettos wore it down.
In this giant room on the last Sunday of the year
Guatemalan grandmothers with impossibly
long braids stuff their clothes into the machines,
a locked determination on their faces,
one more obstacle to fight.
While their children watch cartoons,
squeezed into tiny apartments, as the men
drag home without finding work.
I look around, tall in contrast to the other women.
The washers and dryers chatter noisily,
firing up, shaking their hips, flinging wide their mouths.
Oh the stories they could tell,
if only someone would stop to listen.

The Chair

When its leg broke,
my husband said the chair had to go.
Sent from the kitchen table
before the meal was served
like a child banished for bad behavior.
And what of other discarded objects?
An electric fan on the side of the road.
A stove stripped for parts.
If we look hard enough, will we find
remnants of a marriage scattered in the gutter?
As the fire raced down the hillside behind his house,
my friend fled, taking nothing.
Later, back home, lucky—his house was still standing,
though covered now in soot, front windows blown out—
he considered what he should have grabbed:
the briefcase with passports nestled into the side pocket,
the photo of his father leaning against the archway
of their Cairo home with a cigarette in his hand.
He'd always meant to tell his father to quit.

Bruges

An unusually clean city,
buildings historic, quaint.
But my memories are different.

We moved to Europe after the war
opposite the wave of migration
that thrust the lucky ones onto boats
bound for Ellis Island.

Like the itinerant Jews
of past generations, we too
wandered country to country.
Cities shrunk to postage stamp size.
A series of dingy hotel rooms.
A few months in Oslo, long enough
to start preschool, then on to Paris,
where my brother and I, hands held,
flew an inch off the ground

as my mother ran,
dragging us behind her
like a weak kite, ducking corners
as the Algerian riots engulfed the city.

She boiled everything in Athens,
so afraid I would dip again into illness,
no common language to discuss symptoms
with the doctors. I remained the sickly child.

Scum of burnt milk seeped into the mattress,
even the wool sweaters she bundled us in.
What made my father work for the Marshall Plan?
Some kind of strange repayment for survival?
Scars remained: a quiver in Papa's chin
whenever the Soviet Union was mentioned,

how he refused to speak Russian, his mother tongue.
And the *yahrzeit* candles always burning
on the tiny kitchen counters as we moved around,
for my mother's side wasn't so lucky.
Her grandfather refusing to leave Germany.
America wasn't religious enough, he said.

And now what do I remember of that Bruges?
Not the magnificent remnants of castles
or roofs cut out in the shape of staircases,
not even the pastries drowning in cream.
But the one Bruges painting
in the museum. A man's flesh
peeled back slowly by a hook.
Layers of muscle glisten, a hint
of white bone beneath. He is still alive.
I hear his nerves screaming, even now.

The Icon Painter

A man with no religion
fell in love with the curl of gold leaf.
Each morning he laid down its ribbons,
cutting a halo around the oval face of a saint
with almond eyes and a nose severe as a scolding.
As night descended, he'd tuck in the figure,
pull up the blanket of color around it,
trace the shape of Slavonic letters,
humming the vespers as he battled the darkness.

I met this man at a Russian church in Canada.
I'd crossed the border to lose myself in the vespers,
pulled in by the chants, the swinging brass censer,
wafts of myrrh and pine incense.
A silver iconostasis with latticed vines
dividing the nave from the divine,
the congregants from the black-robed priests.
No one questioned me.

It's been decades since then.
I've gone in and out of my own religion.
Lured by the possibility of solace, but in the end,
cannot follow the rules for long.

Still each time I crack an egg, I think of him.
He became a monk, so he would never
have to leave those tempera paints behind.
I understand that temptation,
those cloistered walls.
Each icon he finishes, a portal to heaven.

Summer of Love

The city shifted under a net of morning fog.
Streets restless as in the wait before
the marionette show at Golden Gate Park
when the audience hunches together for warmth.

She gripped her map, found the narrow Victorian
turquoise as tropical waters, mounted the steps.
When the front door swooned open
the unmarried couple seemed normal enough.

Still she looked around for signs.
Her mother's warning, *There must be something there:*
wineglasses abandoned half full
tumbled sheets glimpsed down the hall.

It was 1967, a city about to burst
its voluptuous seams.
A sheltered girl let loose for a weekend.
She sat on the faded velvet couch, peeked

under the lid of a candy bowl on the coffee table.
Nestled among the peppermints
a pubic hair.
She'd expected this and more.

Statue

On a corner of Pico Blvd.
stands a statue of Christ
palms facing up in supplication.

He has not stirred
the thirty years I have watched him.

What does he want?

I was taught to be afraid.
My mother's family escaped,
while others not so fortunate.
My father beaten up
by Irish boys in Brooklyn
walking to school.

Why did we children need to hear
these stories at the dinner table
between bowls of borscht I sloshed
to the table and platters of kasha
with spikes of mushrooms.

I hated that food.
I wanted white bread so soft
it stuck to the roof of the mouth,
crusts cut off, dignified.
Not what was good for me,
dark grains to put on flesh.

Christ still refuses to move
from that intersection.
His hands must be so tired.
All those years, begging.

Driving Late at Night in Hollywood with a Foreign Visitor

Past the neon signs raw as splinters.
The kid stumbling down the sidewalk
as if unaccustomed to the confinement of shoes.
The tourists taking turns like chess pieces,
snapping photos in front of Graumann's Chinese Theater
to admire back home, settling into a crowded booth
for tea and steamed dumplings.
Past the tattoo parlor that offers more than decoration.
My visitor has never been so tempted.
Movie star maps for sale, smiling posters of all his idols.
Don't get me wrong.
I know we should make a place for Elvis,
but the cracked Naugahyde in the diner is a body falling apart,
the oozing stuffing cries out for stitches.
More than the televangelist can deliver.
He's talking to my visitor.
If only he'd fork over the hard-earned dollars
he'd saved for this vacation.
Go have a drink in Hooters.
The busty waitresses are only college students
trying to earn book money.
Why not appreciate what's God given?
It's getting late, time to drop off my visitor.
He'll unpack, lay the striped shirts his wife
so carefully folded in the long drawer,

pick up the Bible from the nightstand.
It doesn't matter that he can barely speak the language.
There's salvation there.
He only needs to decipher the alphabet.

The Closing

Parishes vanish in PA as laid-off workers go elsewhere.
—*Los Angeles Times*

For years Rose scrubbed the altar
every Tuesday morning, gossiped with the other
women over tea and babka in the church hall.
Pennies hidden at the bottom of her flour bin
for candles on Sunday morning.

Josef, her husband, worked in the mines.
No God in that hellhole, he said as he rubbed
his hands back and forth over his thighs,
to exorcise more than coal dust,
maybe the boss who laughed at his Slovak accent
or standing in line on payday in snow
that was never cleared, except in front
of management offices.

When he got home, after stopping at George's Bar
for one with the boys, there was Rose at the door,
leaning so hard against the frame the paint rubbed off.
She snatched those bills from him,
clutched the coins in her fists, clinked them
into the pocket of the apron she didn't even
bother to pull off before she walked
the three blocks to Holy Trinity Church.

She talks to that statue of Jesus
who's crying over and over again.
Josef hates this.
A grown woman believing in angels.
The light streams onto the angels' sweet faces
through the stained glass windows,
even when the rain slashes in fury.
You should have seen them, she says.
It was beautiful.

Each Time the Doors Open

I've been in many elevators: glass ones that
shoot straight up to the fiftieth floor.
Programmed ones that jerk floor to floor,
awkward as stutterers and so stuffed that
soon you know more than you ever wanted to
about the strangers pressed against you.
Tiny cages so small you can barely stand after
you've dragged in one worn suitcase.

Three floors only in this building but the car won't stop at two.
So you have to thumb a ride to three and walk down.
But on the way up the walls start to pulse, pushing
a man and a woman toward one another, then
pulling them apart, as if they were hitched to opposing pulleys.

This couldn't be what Elisha Graves Otis imagined.
Not in the chapter "Traction Machine" in the repair book
that explains how the friction between the hoists thrusts the car up and up.
How a set of weights rope directly to a winding drum for
counterbalance.
How does the car know how to stop?
This one doesn't, shattering the roof.
There's danger out there and each time
the doors open there is great risk.

This Month in Michigan

Call it exile,

off a rural road named Main, on the edge
of a small lake that chants all night.

At the Dollar Store an empty-handed girl waiting
behind me in line, finally blurts: *Are you hiring?*

She's too young for such a hardened stare,
even with lids half closed, turquoise petals.

The GM factory up Highway 91 out on strike again.
By the roadside the line-workers' placards wobble like loose teeth.

This winter harsh enough to shred barns.
Come spring the rivers will swell till they topple their banks.

Still I seek refuge, optimistic
as those who plant before the last freeze.

An act of faith, as surely as the photos taped to the cash register;
amulets to protect the town's boys from harm in Iraq.

There is so much that threatens an early bloom:
neglect, disease, the before and the after.

The Woman Afraid of Buttons

I never noticed the woman's clothes buttonless,
only the oversized earrings gaudy as a shout,
how her body shrinks beneath them.

Perhaps as a baby
her mother shook her three times,
until her organs shifted in their pockets

her mother's voice ascending
a ladder of panic, the kitchen air slivered
as the infant turned blue.

Now we happen upon one another.
My blouse with its triplets of buttons,
the kind a Victorian lover would stumble over

on the road to the forbidden.

Staring, the woman shudders as she greets me,
turns away. I follow her gaze out into the street
up to the drawer of the sky that darkens

as buttons of hail clatter to the sidewalk.

In Dying Order

for Judy Neveau

The house must be in dying order
said the Swedish aunt.

You must make the bed before leaving.
Not a careless toss of the comforter

to lightly cover rumpled sheets
and quiet the lingering shadows of a dream.

Hospital corners, a blanket stretched tight
so that no secrets are divulged.

Walk room to room
as if you were a potential buyer.

Survey the kitchen counter for errant spills.
Check the refrigerator for odors,

then move silently into the living room.
How old are the magazines on the coffee table?

Strip the potted plant of its browning leaves,
fill the candy dish just below the top.

Lock the door on your way out.
It might be your last time and you want

to leave everything as it should be, so that
after the accident, when your body is broken

at least your house will be in order.
It will make you proud.

The Spiral

Let us examine the augers* of warm waters.
270 species, some with barbed teeth
that shoot poison to subdue their prey.
The victim, paralyzed, consumed whole.
On Cape Verde, islanders attached augers
to sticks, harnessed them as darts for blowguns.
A display as ingenious as it is cruel.

Think of the manifestation of form.
The flight path of mockingbird
in the shape of a pearly nautilus.
Such a bounty of shells.
Flat spirals and sundials improbably tall.
The iridescent moon snail.
Even predatory, carnivorous snails have their use.
Is the wentletrap the most graceful of gastropods?
Oh their many ribbed whorls,
thickened lips transform to a rib-like varix.

Once you believe in spirals
you see them everywhere: your firstborn
as Slinky winding his way in the world,
until unemployment snaps him back to the home nest.
The former friend as box crab (enemy of the auger)
who uses his pincers to clip back the lip of shell
to reach the animal inside, gnawing at the tender flesh.

* a kind of mollusk

Jellyfish

I've never understood belief
why some Catholics are lapsed, as if they haven't
used their library cards in due time and will lose
their privileges, be branded for life as nonreaders.
Or that belief was a kind of social security number
you could look up if you needed it for an application.
I've watched those films
when the preacher dunks a sinner in a lake and
the supplicant bobs up, shaking off the water,
the sins flung into orbit.
I know plenty about guilt,
but have never understood what it is to be saved.
Do you have to forfeit or can you hedge your bets
and know ahead of time what the reward will be?
I'll put my faith in jellyfish.
Having no respiratory system would be a plus.
Mine is nothing but trouble; I cough and people back away
flinging me the evil eye, as if I were a danger to society.
I want an umbrella body that
contracts and pulses, a minuet of the ocean, repeating
the melody in inventive patterns, circling backwards,
then shooting toward the surface in a miracle of motion.
My nerve net would respond to sunlight.
I'd gladly be swept into a bloom
of moon jellyfish, a ghostly mass thumping like blood.
Or succumb to a swift current that sweeps me
from the Pacific to the coast of Africa.
If you're underwater, what happens if a trout swims by,
scales silver, pointillist spots gleaming?
Wouldn't you want to follow it?
Even sturgeon can be beautiful.

III

Eating Crow

Sing a song of sixpence a pocket full of rye,
Four and twenty blackbirds baked in a pie.
When the pie was opened the birds began to sing . . .

On TV the *Bizarre Foods* host leans over
a rickety market stall in Bangkok.
He picks at the toothpick bones of a sparrow,
licks his lips and reaches for a second bird,
its skeleton the size of his palm.

A cook to a medieval knight would place
live birds inside a pastry crust.
A great joke, though the real pie was served
after the birds had been released.

Is that how we got the four and twenty blackbirds
whose heads pop through a blanket of pie crust?
Beaks wide to sing their hearts out,
though they are cooked through and through.

In the Middle Ages, peafowl was served
on any table worth its weight.
The birds decked out in a mantle of herbs,
green as a king's velvet collar.

The steer's head displayed like
crown jewels on the butcher table
put me off meat that year in Russia,
but no more than the intestines
ladled into a pond of broth.

I may succumb to the occasional hamburger.
Still I wanted to rescue those little birds
from their pinched cages before
they met their deaths in a bath of oil.
To take the fingers of the food show host,
smack them away, before he licked them clean.

Sea Monsters

From the time I first crossed the Atlantic by ship
I have believed in sea monsters.
Much as a man prays to a God
he does not see, I knew they were there
gliding beneath the waves, watching us.

Now in High Plains country, the ice-crusted hills
shift their eyes as I drive late at night,
the only car on a dirt road.
The earth pulls apart, two hinges
swinging on a trap door.

Fissures open to an evaporating sea.
Tidal flats ooze red, the water drops
and floodplains emerge.
Spruce lurk at the bottom of Jenny Lake.
The land flattens in a sigh.
You can see for miles, a stubble of snow on the slopes.

How can you say there are no sea monsters
when we have the proof in drawings:
the nine-headed hydra or a creature with the
mane of a horse and the body of a coiled serpent?
Deep in this sediment and crystalline rock
claws stretch, a tooth hangs over a lip.

Say I Believe

Once upon a time there lived a king and queen whose fondest wish had come true: they had been blessed with a baby girl.

Snatching babies is best
Done after dark is less
Risky if the kidnapper
Masquerades as a woman
Eases entry into the house
Where the cradle ideally beech or
Pine when an amulet hangs in the
Corner light illuminates the
Mother of God cannot be extinguished
The nun declared as a Jew I cannot
Say I believe in any of this still
My mother would not allow me to
Purchase the stroller ahead of
The day my pregnancy was announced
The rabbi's wife brought me a card
Two lions and a hamsa* to ward
Off the evil eye pierce a lemon with nails
Drip olive oil into water beware
Dark-haired Lilith perched on the sill
Waiting for the ideal time to snatch the baby
After she is bathed and fed she is
Happiest now she has turned eighteen and
Has left me, probably

* picture (amulet) of a hand

A Scattering of Stones

In the shadow of bombed-out windows, crumbling stairs,
I was sucked into the wind tunnel of the Brothers Grimm,
where an old woman with an outstretched palm piled
with striped candies enticed just such a girl as I.
The stepsisters who hacked off their heels,
blood dripping on the floorboards
as they hobbled toward the court messenger
to squeeze into the glass slipper.
Warning signs I knew, yet ignored years later.
When the phone rang, a man's satin voice beckoned.
As if in a trance, I succumbed; followed
the breadcrumbs to his house.
I pushed open the back gate, as foolish as any heroine.

A desolate garden is more seductive than a fertile one.
Such possibilities ripe for invention!
I closed my eyes and the sad stubble of lawn
turned brilliant with lampposts of daisies.
A scattering of stones framed the border.
Spikes of blue salvia enough to hold onto,
even a pond with a golden fish to predict the future.
Sometimes we get what we wish for.
This is always dangerous.
I slip on the brocaded gown,
let down my hair, but he does not return.

Before Dark

Up the road just before
Dark the clouds flatten
The horizon shaped as a
Mattress hoarding wire
Lances the porcupine's
Quills of branches
Pierce the gunpowder sky
Cinches at the edges of
Hunger the wind slapping
Night against the valley
Walls, the clawing hunger

Lullaby

Although the rattler startled in the
bathroom sink that July is hibernating,
last night's clicking was not the wind
slapping against Big Horn Mountain
but the rattler pulsing its tail, dreaming
of that steel basin warmed by the sun.

You used up one life that day.
The charm not guaranteed to last.
Snakes and spiders can still escape
your childhood books to find you.
Who was this Mother Goose?
Queen Bertha, mother of Charlemagne,
with webbed feet? Or the other Bertha,
wife of Robert II of France, whose baby
sprouted the head of a goose?
Perhaps the American, Elizabeth Foster Goose,
stepmother to ten, mother to six:
Baby, baby, naughty baby,
Hush you squalling thing I say.

A woman I know put an amulet under
each child's pillow so he would not
be snatched by wild geese.
When she turned her head,
the children grew up,
traveled abroad,
leaving her forever.

Fire Ant

I cannot say what drew me to the mirror or what I expected:
That my right eye had bargained with the left to switch places

I meant it no harm
Though recognized it as a messenger

A spell to conjure the call which so far had not
Broken the air in a cascade of quarter notes

I could have flung it off
But transfixed by its six quivering legs

Even the mailbox was empty, though I thrust my fist deep into its belly
Unfolding the wings of my fingers to trace the four sides

I watched it poised to bite
The sting from its abdomen left a tattoo

I counted the three steps down the stone stairs onto the garden path
A fire ant surfaced from a small dome, wobbled its way

Through the damp grass toward me, copper-brown head visible
It was carrying a message if only I would squat down to receive it

An angry volcano burst on my upper arm
Its venom the sign I was waiting for

New Math

My mother was a math whiz
triple digits, four columns.
Addition slid from her tongue
like a native language.
Division, subtraction,
it made no difference.
Quadruple a number, halve it.
A branch snapping midway
in an ice storm.
No room for dullards who
could not discern the difference
between squared and doubled.
I barricaded behind fairy tales.
The Green Book faded into *The
Yellow* on my nightstand.
The Red Book filled with blood,
a finger pricked on a spindle,
eyes gouged out by thorns.
She'd pose a question,
I'd close my eyes, reach for a number
believing in its salvation.
It's been a long time since she died.
Even numbers couldn't save her,
though she survived double digits
past all expectations.
With a calculator I get by,
hiding my defect.
No more smearing the pencil
across squares of graph paper.
My lover asked for one hundred love poems,

but could not wait past ten.
On the seventeenth week, he drew a line
in permanent marker to calculate.
Tallied up the score at ten poems,
threw a couple of singles on the table,
numbers left over from long division.
That will have to do.
He's got to move on.
There's trigonometry, then calculus.
No stopping him now.

Defying Gravity

The boy runs up the down escalator defying gravity.
His father stands below, hands flickering
like a sphinx moth in a web of slender branches.
He pleads with his son to come down.

A woman glances sideways, a hint of smile.
She thinks about the small thrills of danger readily abandoned.
Even beets persist in bleeding on the clean countertop.
Breath and touch.

Outside clouds break and gather like the joining
of hands in prayer, if one believes that.
Faith has never come to me,
though I long for the granting of wishes.

The young couple with arms linked, not in battle.
Swish of a pony's mane, muscles twitching.
Hooves scratch from inside a picture frame.

A child hoisted up by his father's muscular arms
before the saddle disintegrates
and the color bleaches to nothing.
Before another year dissolves into the trampled grass.

Guy Fawkes Day

Remember, remember the fifth of November,
Gunpowder, treason and plot.

Berries snapped on the pyre and the flames erupted.
The bonfire full blast, yet men threw on more branches,
three steps forward, two paces back,
a dance form I could not name.
I didn't know who Guy Fawkes was or
even the meaning of treason.
No one had bothered to explain these things to a child
newly arrived in a country full of mystery:
bangers and mash, elevenses, an English I did not recognize.
But flames already haunted me.

I had heard the whispered stories;
we had lost relatives in the war.
In my child's mind, all incinerators burned,
so those back home were the same.
Though they appeared harmless, I knew
their bellies were crammed with secrets.

Even the curtains in my room conspired against me.
Profiles of burglars emerged from the stripes,
their faces all menace, eyes hooded.
Burrowing under the blankets was only temporary protection.

When we landed in England, I was ill-prepared
for that November night when my schoolmates
made a man, stuffing a shirt and trousers of their fathers' old clothes.
The men hoisted the effigy higher and higher.
Soon the figure would catch on the moon, causing it
to lose its balance and tumble into the flames.

We leaned back to squint in anticipation of the destruction.
With a grunt, the ropes slackened and Guy Fawkes dropped.
My palms burned all that year with gunpowder.

Instruction in Witchcraft

Grimm and his brother had it right
in the story where the evil woman
opened her mouth to tell lies and instead
out hopped a frog, then another and another.
Imagine the webbed toes sinking
into the fleshy tongue, the slime
of frog skin coating the inside of a cheek.

Start the witchcraft slowly, casually.
When your enemy is lunching
at a lacey table piled high
with tea sandwiches, command
a small stain to surface
on her linen pants. As she dabs,
will it to quietly double in size.

The next week the limb of an old maple
crashes, narrowly missing her
but hitting her new car.
The hood collapses like a crushed fist.
She might tell her friends
the tree was diseased and she extremely lucky,
but that's not true, is it?

Later to calm herself she prepares
homemade lasagna, takes a generous
forkful expecting the tang of tomatoes,
the comfort of wide noodles.
Instead something wiggles on her teeth.

She extracts a fat worm. A second one idles
down her chin, plopping into her lap.

Deliver the tour de force at a cocktail party
where she wears a body-hugging dress, red.
She laughs, tells jokes.
Her necklace pure gold, strung with
diamonds gaudy as Christmas lights.
It tightens after each sentence,
imperceptibly at first. No one else notices.

London Bridge

London Bridge is falling down,
My fair lady.

My father read aloud
at the breakfast table about a teenaged girl who jumped
the night before from the Golden Gate Bridge.
I was a child, already waking
from nightmares of failed flight across the bay, dipping down
into the churning waves.

The girl climbs the red skeleton of the bridge,
her hand curls around the cables, then her fist opens.
London Bridge harbors
its own dark history. They say a virgin
was sacrificed in its construction.
Viking invaders burned
the bridge down. Lot's wife turned to look at Sodom.
Flesh to salt. Wood to stone. Water wheels ground the grain.
Pushed by the Thames' flow.
Wood and clay will wash away, wash away. Wood and clay
will wash away, My fair lady.

Lead, tin, iron, copper.
Could the girl have been saved? Talked down
from the tightrope?
The old London Bridge
was dismantled in the 1960s, shipped stone by stone
to Lake Havasu, Arizona.

When we played London Bridge
the boys tightened their wires of arms around us girls. We were locked
in; for all we knew, it would be a lifelong ending.
Lead to gold, copper to silver.
Iron and steel will bend and bow, bend and bow. Iron and steel
will bend and bow, My fair lady.

The Insomniac

Give him a noun at three a.m.
one syllable to chew on
two to wrestle meat from bone
to sharpen the incisors

The sun rises over and over
for those who don't succumb
to the tide of sleep
who reject the dreams that circle

Numbers from a list of
unfinished projects tap him on the shoulder
Phone calls not returned to his mother
The walls begin to inch their way to his bed

To float does not require sleep
The weeds grow all night
whether watched over or abandoned
Parked cars trade gossip under the stare of porch lights

And if sleep never returns
eyelids half-lowered blinds
the mind chatters like a record stuck in its groove
thoughts hammer out the rhythm

Clouds sharpen after midnight
unafraid of stalkers who target his corner house
Insomnia shreds his sentences
a tearing apart of the mind   his right hand a fist pounding
All night the rote stutter of his kitchen clock

IV

The Art of the Stitch

On the lid of a seventeenth-century box, Queen Esther pleads with open
palms
to the King. She understood a woman's power, for on the back panel
Haman swings from scaffolding,

hardly a suitable subject for needlepoint.
Other chair cushions illustrate the scandalous tale of King Solomon
and the Queen of Sheba, shown in various stages of undress.

Peering through glass on the third floor of a brownstone museum,
I am drawn to a lone tree on a box made to hold a lady's toiletries,
the tree where Charles II hid from Cromwell. I remember the family
pilgrimage

to Shropshire to view that oak. At eight I worried there were not enough
leaves
to hide the king, as if I could have saved him or my own relatives
whose fate my parents discussed when I was supposed to be asleep.

Now I petition for help: Teach me the art of the stitch:
French knot, ladder stitch, double cross; to learn
from the pattern maker the necessity of choice;

to master the art of the knot and tie down the pieces;
to snip and discard mistakes.

Let me unearth gold thread and silk cord,
trace the tail of a partridge, give it substance,
then set the bird free.

Bleak with Trees

1\.

What would you have bid on, if you could?
An antler wine rack waiting to be reunited with its head?
The cane with a bone handle carved by an old ranch hand?
Or the divining rod that for years has failed to find
water in this remote Wyoming valley?

2\.

My friend hauled out a heat lamp each October
the two years she lived in a farmhouse in Maine.
She stretched out on her couch practicing for the coffin.
Phone calls from friends could not protect her from the dark
but the coils of heat and burning light rescued her.

3\.

This morning, scraps of snow, the hillside a cowboy's
cheek with a scruffy beard of silver sagebrush.
His shaving hand no longer trustworthy, the razor's path
on his chin traces the geography of the moon with
patches of dark stubble rising from it.

4\.

If I could choose any location, I'd take bleak with trees,
silhouetted mountains, a gulley for porcupines.
This high desert with its sumac and bitterbrush scares me.
Nowhere to hide; just look up Highway 14 at Crazy Shirley's
with her four shacks, three horses and too many cars to count.

5.

I've made mistakes, run away repeatedly in another language.
For years I've pushed in vain against solid doors.
Maybe those first months confined to an incubator launched me
on the wrong path; now I'd choose shadow over those lights.
A prairie view, my salvation.

Career Change

She wants to change careers:
trade in her research on drug abuse,
county meetings that stretch
for decades, even the corner office perks.

She tours California's waterways
with a group of geologists.
Seduced by the lure of tectonic mixing,
sediment swept onto continents,
the downhill transport
of particles: sand, silt, mud.

Evaporation and rainfall,
leaf litter, iron and clay.
All that soil waiting for her.

She rubs thumb to index finger
as if brushing off loose clumps.
The dirt transforms to coal,
her high heels disintegrate into work boots.
The snakes, the scorpions,
blazing heat on her bending back
as she squints, hunting for something
she cannot name—
she'll take it all.

Singer and His Sewing Machine

Isaac Merritt Singer's story is a better read
than any owner's manual:
Married at nineteen in New York,
he grew restless with a wife and baby,
joined a theater as a booking agent,
then climbed onto the stage as a hero, a cad.
Maybe it was the plays that did it,
an audience to worship him.

In Baltimore he proposed marriage again.
Soon he had two wives and two children.
Singer created the straight line,
but never learned its lesson.
Though he looped in circles,
he willed the shuttle to thrust up and down.

Overhanging arm, straight eye needle,
a presser foot to secure the cloth:
he bequeathed precision to women everywhere.
Something to rely on, while his own embroidery unraveled.
Singer added a third wife, this time in Paris,
six more children followed.

Now there are machines for every need:
one-step buttonholes, see-through bobbins,
an automatic needle threader.
Model 7463 is called Confidence.
Model 7436, Ingenuity.
I'll take one of each.

Spillville

After two years in New York
Dvorak and his family traveled
by rail to Spillville, Iowa.
Eleven hours they journeyed before being
deposited at the station in Calmar.
Then six more miles by carriage
to their final destination.
In New York Dvorak was homesick.
He longed to find comfort in Iowa
for the next hundred days, with his wife,
Anna, and six children, sixteen on down.
So eager was he to be accepted
that he memorized the names of
the townspeople, so he could greet
each one as he passed their homes.
This was not so hard, as they were all Czech,
save one German, one Swiss and one Norwegian.
But all the residents thought Dvorak a little mad,
for on his first morning there, he heard something
he had not heard in eight months: a bird call,
a red black-winged tanager, whose song
would soon haunt his new string quartet.
In his excitement he walked straight to
St. Wenceslas Catholic Church,
sat down at the organ, startling
the old women in the pews below.
He thundered out "Lord, Before Thy Mercy"
until the stone walls shook in reverberation
and the old women's tongues clicked and
rattled in their houses of bone and flesh.

Merce Cunningham and the Music

He uses chance procedures—dice-rolling, coin-
flipping—to decide many crucial things.

Merce Cunningham knows it's best
to decide by not deciding.
So he rolls the dice and there are
six parts to a new dance;
twenty dots translate into minutes per section.

It's perfect if you think about it.
Flip tails and one male dancer will appear
stage left, heads and a female will jump from stage right.
Everything sorted this way:

how many dancers, even the score,
if you could call the collision of stick
on metal, sound.
And his famous sixty-seven-minute silence,
is this music too?

Chance becomes its own order,
reinventing itself at each performance.

A square of arm intertwines
with a circle of torsos, forming an embrace.
Cunningham ordered it all, but if
the die flips to one, the lights go dark,
the smeared backdrop raised.

And the dancers?
At the Brooklyn Academy of Music,

Cunningham apologized.
They had not been able to rehearse.
He would work it out in front of the audience.
He gave the die to one dancer who rolled a four.
So on with the sets, the costumes.
Just watch.
Two chance throws can explode into
thirty-two different combinations.
Do the math.

On a Stretch of Coastline

Squeezed on both sides by four stripes of wire, barbs snapping
in the wind like the wicked fairy's come hither,

the lane collapses into the largest lagoon in the Lower 48
where forty years ago the water rose, tracing a figure eight

through downtown, sweeping eleven people out to sea.
Even now the town drowns its sorrows beneath a battering of rain,

families split raw between developers and nature lovers,
while an endangered butterfly (the lotus blue), hides in stretches

of drying bog, or (depending on your beliefs) is now extinct.
At sundown fishermen haul up half-empty crab cages, then disperse to
rundown bars

to drink their way through another punishing winter.
Ink-stained clouds push against the mountains like children

shoving on a playground. I swear I wouldn't be alone if I escaped here too
into the forest to pick wild blackberries, leaving no forwarding address.

Lucy Bakewell Audubon Sets the Record Straight

It was fair my father at first did not
release me to marry our young neighbor from France.
After he fell into a creek and contracted fever,
I nursed John James Audubon back to health.
Then he returned to Europe to ask for his own father's blessing.
He studied the art of taxidermy, stuffed snakes and opossums.
I too love the wilds of this country, from the Kentucky hills
to the western fringes with their bonanza pines and bristeberry.
After John returned home to start a general store, we married.
The following year, the first of our two sons was born.
This started the bad spell: I lost two baby girls, Lucy and Rose.
Can a mother ever recover the loss of her babies?
Then the rats ate John's drawings, over two hundred of them.
I worked as a chambermaid, tutored plantation girls.
I knew what I had to do.
My husband set sail for England in 1826 and stayed three years.
Dressed in moccasins, a tomahawk hanging from his belt,
he was the darling of the Continent.
With his life-sized drawings of birds and tales of Indians,
he regaled his hosts in drawing rooms, sold portraits
of young ladies for five dollars apiece.
I begrudge him none of this.
But oh I waited for an invitation to join him!
And oh I wait for his acknowledgment still!

The Anatomy of a Palm and the Confluence of Lines

Even after a night of storms
left the chorus of palms
that guard the boulevard
bereft of limbs,
the sidewalk strewn with fronds,
still the trees do not complain,
instead cradle their aching joints.
No deaths even in the saplings that
sprouted beside the matriarchs.
Up the length of their bodies,
each checks for breakage
in the spinal column.
A vertebra rotated in a spiral,
the ring of fiber disc cracking.
The honeycomb of its bone tissue sags.
No question of collision in
the intersection of trajectories.
This aftermath of nature's wrath.
What do they expect,
living so close to the ocean?
Where even a concrete wall
is no match for the cycle of destruction.
Still they stand in stubborn determination.
The strength of the trunks sorely
tested in last night's winds.
So the assessment begins.
Who down the line has suffered no damage,
bending instead to the angle of the curve

as the rain beat against the torso?
A matter of survival to maintain
the perpendiculars of the spine
to its transverse axis.
At their point of intersection,
a confluence of lines.

Leonard Bernstein Speaks to Me

Ten p.m. I drag myself to the car.
Even the security booth is abandoned.
I slide in, check the backseat, lock the doors.
So dark I cannot fit the key into its hole.
The engine grumbles,
roused unhappily from its slumber.
On the radio a man lectures on the symphony.
It is Lennie, a voice I have known since childhood.

Lennie, tell me more, that everything will turn around.
Money appear in my bank account, a discovered concerto.
Creditors dropped like a revised score.
The Largo waiting to catch me before I fall.
Let me understand how the world is larger than a symphony,
such intricate parts, the delight of a piccolo,
the torrent of kettledrum.
Let me follow your baton as you gather up the violins,
whip them into a crescendo, rein them in,
calm them, then fool them into submission.

Chocolate and the Afterlife

She wrote of it as no one had: of the men who picked the pods, dried the beans, ground the nibs, walked home trailing a scent from the walls of Hansel and Gretel, all the way to the Aztecs and Mayans. She hovered in kitchens, dipped her fingers in blackened pots, stacked the recipes, shuffled them skillfully as a poker player. Her cookbook was proclaimed the bible of all bibles. It bought her the land, built the house, paid for a redwood deck, polished to the color of cinnamon. But restlessness nipped at her. Travel caught her in its hot air balloon. Chocolate soufflés deflated as she moved on. Next a stampede of wolfhounds with eyes one step from the tundra. She trusted them. Whippets sleek as shadows moved in; she rescued borzois, found homes for the neglected. Any four-legged creature, even as she abandoned friends. I hadn't seen her for years when I got the call, standing at the counter chopping dill. I'll rifle my cupboard for bitter chocolate, melt it down, pour it from on high, a dark river to the afterlife.

Cobbler from Yerevan

We lean on either side of the chipped counter as he rotates my shoes.
Always enough and never he answers, though I've yet to ask a question.
He glances at the television, half expecting help.
Scraps of words tumble from his mouth in English and Russian.
I'm limping along, trying to keep up, but when
he lapses into default Armenian, he loses me.
Maybe it doesn't matter, only that I listen as he pauses
to count his sorrows: the wait each Sunday at the prison,
his oldest son busted for drugs, so many years wasted.
If he'd stayed in the old country, he'd be slapping worn-out shoes
with new soles made of salvaged tires.
His wife would prepare pilaf with fresh herbs,
a little meat, strong mint tea to wash it down.
She'd squeeze shut her eyes to will her children home for supper.
Now the cobbler flicks his forehead, frowning.
You can only look back for so long.

Copper and Steel

It remains a mystery
how the turning of a spigot
releases the flow
Water brought forth by sheer will
or blind trust
We must pay homage to the pipes
force of their angles
the resilience of curves
as if sheer determination
could bend steel
So much taken for granted
We recoil at a trickle of rust
as if there were danger in it
Perhaps it is better to love a plumber
than a poet
Reach for a Stanley wrench
to tighten an elbow joint
before the copper rod bursts
and the water rises

The Apple

Before, a plucked apple had to be tied down
to prevent the wings of its leaves
from taking flight.

In late spring the sky filled with fruit,
dark orbs of plums swayed on spindled branches.
Peaches swirled in elaborate minuets
chased by clusters of cherries.

Nabbing and fastening took hours.
The mistress of the house
wrote out elaborate schedules,
posted them in the kitchen:

First the manservant with a butterfly net,
next the housemaid with a basket for the catch,
even the cook impatient to prepare
pie and jam for afternoon tea.

One day Isaac Newton meandered
in his mother's Lincolnshire garden.
An apple fell, not rising to the moon,
as it had until then.

He knelt on the ground, scooped it up
where it slept in his palm.
This marked the end of one world, the beginning of another.
Like Adam, he bit into the apple, the juice running down his chin.

About the Author

Carol V. Davis received the 2007 T. S. Eliot Prize for Poetry for *Into the Arms of Pushkin: Poems of St. Petersburg* (Truman State University Press). She is the author of *It's Time to Talk About…*, published in a bilingual collection in Russia (1997), and two chapbooks, *Letters From Prague* and *The Violin Teacher*. She was a senior Fulbright scholar in Russia in 1996/97 and 2005. Her poetry has been read on National Public Radio and Radio Russia, and at the Library of Congress. She was the 2008 Poet-in-Residence at Olivet College in Michigan and currently teaches at Santa Monica College in California.